Time Gentlemen, Please

KEVIN HIGGINS

salmonpoetry

Published in 2008 by
Salmon Poetry,
Cliffs of Moher, County Clare, Ireland
Website: www.salmonpoetry.com
Email: info@salmonpoetry.com

ISBN 978-1-903392-76-8

Cover artwork: Maev Lenaghan
Cover design & typesetting: Siobhán Hutson

"Eventually, Kevin will grow up."

Councillor Nadia Conway, Mayor of Enfield
in *The Enfield Advertiser*, July 22nd 1993

"There are no messiahs,
just some very naughty boys."

Darrell Kavanagh, former Militant Labour candidate
for Latymer Ward, Edmonton, The London Borough of Enfield,
January 1st, 2008

Acknowledgments

Acknowledgements are due to the following magazines, chapbooks and anthologies in which some of these poems first appeared:

Poetry Ireland Review, The Sunday Tribune, Magma, Fortnight, The Shop, Metre, Orbis, The Burning Bush, West 47, ROPES, The Recorder (New York), *The Antigonish Review* (Canada), *Vallum* (Canada), *Coal City Review* (Kansas), *Crannóg, The Cúirt Annual, The Argotist* (online), *Galway Xposed, The Private Review* (online), *Nthposition.com, Moloch E-zine, The Brobdignagian Times, Markings, Poetry Nottingham International, XYZ* (New York), *Dublin Quarterly* (online), *Harvest International* (Los Angeles), *Iota, Aesthetica, Westword, Criterion, New Left Journal, Oasis, Indite Circle* (online), *The Stony Thursday Book, Seam, The Black Mountain Review, Poetry Monthly, The Stinging Fly, Obsessed With Pipework, Fusebox* (online), *Braquemard, Book in Canada: The Canadian Review of Books* & *Salmon: A Journey In Poetry 1981-2007*.

The text of 'Summer Interlude' was displayed as part of the *People and Nature* photography exhibition organised by NUI Galway and Galway County Council in August 2006.

'Keyser Soze Does Not Frighten Me' was broadcast on *The Sean Moncrieff Show*, Newstalk Radio.

I would also like to thank The Arts Council of Ireland for the Literature Bursary they awarded me in 2005, which enabled me to take time out to work on some of these poems.

Contents

ONE
From the future, a postcard home

TWO
Ponders End

THREE

Firewood

FOUR
A New City

FIVE
Last Testament

ONE

From the future, a postcard home

To Sunday Evening

Morning slick as a tabloid supplement,
its glad anthem of eggs and bacon.
But then things slipping off the agenda
the network not responding, please try again later
tossing us out through the afternoon: its shut shops,
sad bottle-banks, belts of weather edging in from
the Midlands, bringing long spells, brief interludes;
to the place where you undeniably loom,
like a vicious rumour turning out to be true.

Foreboding

Once more
the endless Monday to Sunday
and back around again, the days
content mostly just to be
a small dog peeing against the same old tree.
So why then do you get the feeling
that the future's about to leap at you,
like a baboon with a hatchet
from a man-hole or a closet, screaming
something which can only mean
'This is the end of the old regime'?

From the future, a postcard home

After the imagined ice-cream clouds
and warm blue rain, the frost bristling
picturesque grass, the parties
where the women were topless, the men
all wearing tuxedos; each day's

metallic tap-water taste. Outside
the chapped lips and tea-cosy hats
of a Winter afternoon's typical trajectory.
In your head, these dissonant fingers
still plinking along with some mad monologue
banging its gong. Outside

the freezing fog bothering their nostrils.
In your head, the essential details
of an August evening: the angle
of her bra-strap as the books
came tumbling, the minus signs

massing at the border. Elsewhere
nothing now but the present
as the cat gives up sniffing your sad
cheeseless hands, and goes back
to catching the giant mice
of its dreams.

The Interruption

After dinner Woodlouse and I take
our cigars to the balcony, and survey
the Bikini coast of his new life; as he tells me how
his brother the PhD is now
a distinguished epidemic
named Theodore, and just last year

his father, in the aftermath
of his lizard Caligula's apparent
suicide, instead of counselling
went for cancelling, and during the third session
vanished altogether... When a car-door
somewhere interjects,

and then a voice tragic from below:
"But Agatha! How could you!?"
And in an instant our cigars
are making their excuses;
while outside baby birds plop
pink and dead from their nests;
as the world hums to itself its song:
Nothing the same again from this day on.

Last Man Standing

In your memory, I talk about how great it was.
Though it didn't happen, and I wasn't there.
The girls we knew were the sort
one minute you're being introduced to them,
the next you're standing on a gallows
in Baghdad, wondering how you got there.
The mornings we woke up laughing,
that year we had nothing to lose.
Though it didn't happen, and I wasn't there.

Before I discovered there is a God, and He's
a balding former Congressman for Wyoming; told you
Rebellion is a place the good pass through,
while the ghastly stay forever. And you replied
that with my Guaranteed Irish smirk and the constant
Hitler-Stalin pact thing I had going on, I was in danger
of becoming everyone's compromise candidate.
Though it didn't happen, and I wasn't there.
In your memory, I talk about how great it was.
Then turn to face the aggressively average day.

The Great Escape

For four days in August
to this place of novelty haircuts
and Surrealist sandcastles.
In weather that once spelt
Socialist Summer Camp
you watch a lone goose
move high across the water;
imagine the wetsuits plopping,
one by one, from a distant rock
are a cult come here
to commit mass suicide. *Kilkee,*
host town to Uzbekistan.
A B&B run by a guy, you're sure
is ex-Romanian army.
The Gold Sea Chinese Takeaway.
Fry-ups all day
until three. You could do this:

whittle yourself a pipe
from a piece of driftwood,
spend the wide autumn evenings
smoking it;
let the terrorists in the television
take over the airports;
just whitter away about how
the man with the metal detector,
who prowls the beach each afternoon,
is definitely working for Them.

Time Gentlemen, Please

Again your head full of novels
you'll definitely get down on paper
one of these days. And Prague? Budapest?
Hemingway or Che? The same old questions
(only a little bit less) night after night
for years. Until all that remains
are a few old acquaintances
over hot whiskeys whispering:
"Not quite here, yet not quite there.
His life just a fence he got piles sitting on":
as through the mild October streets
your hearse makes haste.

The Couple Upstairs

Your husband's last set of golf-clubs
in their vest of cobwebs; and the chair
you've sat in since Jimmy Carter
often empty now, as you tumble away to a life
of medicine, mash and Sunday night
nephews. Moments though

when every sound upstairs
is sex: every rustle across a table-top
some ecstasy of underwear
whistling to the floor, every whisper
of a floorboard her once again, turning
her pale backside to the sky; times

when all he has to do is drop
his *Penguin Book of Poetry From*
Britain and Ireland Since 1945
and you shudder at the thought of them
about to commit an unnatural act
on a Tuesday afternoon. And your stick's

suddenly frantic against the ceiling,
or you're ringing the bell
to tell them to stop, 'til you settle
back to a big, black afterwards now
fractured only by this last lightning
across its sky.

Tuesday

Her still away and the town
all East winds and tonsillitis, as you come
back for a quiet night in not playing
with yourself, but instead get the loud
catastrophe of a friend, whose wife's
finally told him: "Time for Teletubbie fuck off",
meowing on your garage roof. Hours
then of him determined to see nothing
in the coffee cup but the absence now
of anyone to help him to the exit
in the event of darkness. Later,

his blood black with caffeine and whiskey,
he swears on *The Koran, Bible*
and *Little Book of Complete Bollocks* to be more
from now on than an instrument
in any woman's orchestra. And suddenly all you can see
is the promise for him of a long future
of cough syrup and scoreless draws, as he goes on
to share various caravans with guys
with mad, grey, heavy metal hair and perhaps
once a year have an out of underpants experience
with a woman twice his age. By midnight

you're about to tell him
you'd rather wake up with
the late Leonid Brezhnev, than have to listen
to any more of this, but at the last moment
keep your sympathetic head, because
as the proverb says: "Mock not, for tomorrow
you too may have your bare arse
turned to the sun."

No Words

Since the morning she told you
that when you talk
she increasingly hears no words
just loud, continuous
farting; and you took

your striped jacket, your system
of nicknames into that white
February day, with the eyes
of a politician who has no-one to tickle
his Ballinasloe Electoral Area; it's been

bread toasted on a three-bar fire,
the soup of the day
cabbage & whiskey as the insects
take over the house, and you try

to console yourself with the thought
that every time a door closes,
a cat-flap somewhere opens.

On Hearing You've Donated Your Body To Medical Science

after Stevie Smith

Your shoes' commonsense clip-clop shuffle,
that voice like seagulls and muscles clenching,
those small, manageable, flat-chested dreams;

how you remained upstanding
as a novice's nightdress while all around
were losing theirs; and someone comparing you

to a wet Tuesday afternoon. Then the kitchen tiles
one by one tumbling, the peeling linoleum.
The father who took forever to die. This is what

they'll think of, what they'll remember
the day Death finally waltzes you
down the corridor to that dark
laboratory.

Today

When the morning's a letter
which should never have been sent,
the afternoon a fat man sitting
on all your best laid plans, when
—all day long—you're the wrong hand
on the wrong knee with a knack
of turning nothing into even less
and the woman sitting next to you
suddenly runs out screaming; what can you do
but close the curtains on all this,
hope you'll step out of the shower tomorrow
put on your sombrero as usual
and run laughing up Shop Street in the rain,
today turning out to have been
just someone else's horrible dream?

Forecast

Tomorrow your panicking hands as you watch
      your life's furniture float away
through impossible summer rain.
      Your worldly possessions
gathered together in an almost empty plastic bag.
      The changed wind's devastating wit.

But today you still busy putting your teeth in
      around five to eleven in the morning,
and then leaning back in that chair
      as if your bowels are about
to shout: "This is your Captain speaking!"

      Underlings and enemies
around water-coolers everywhere gathering
      to listen to the forecast
and wait for more organised weather.

Room Overlooking The Lake

You there in the back row, third from right, class of 1975,
back when the world was busy telling long jokes
in the college bar, or chanting slogans
in support of the Bolivian Tree People
or the Mothers Of The Disappointed; the one who knew
where he was going and went, smooth
as mustard being spread across an old man's head,
to that Civil Service pension
and all those lunch-times spent munching
onion sandwiches and watching
as the dole-queues came and went,
like weeds. The rest of us still skulking

on and off various trains, or forever crouched
behind the couch the day the rent-man came around,
and you already a man
any forty year old woman would've been proud
to bring home to her mother: that briefcase guaranteed
to make it through all those evening streets
and pairs of slippers to a priest one day whispering:
"ashes to ashes, dust to dust, life not changed,
merely ended." This is what, to a man, we predicted.
Not the gin for dinner, the whiskey
across your Corn Flakes. The wife giving up on you
the day you started putting

hard-boiled eggs under the mattress
'just to see what would happen'.
Later you looking like death cooled down
as you stood on the street corner crooning
"Love Me Tender." And now being led
into the back of an ambulance ranting:
"long live the rotten old consensus!", then going off through
the pale hatchet-faced afternoon
to another basket-weaving class, another game
of dominos in that room overlooking the lake.

Somewhere Else

Better to risk it
and see if the Missouri woods
really are, as you say, patrolled
by snakes with AK47s,
hissing: "Are you from somewhere else?";
than spend my halcyon decades
whispering down the usual street
towards a plate of ham sandwiches
in the room above the local pub, the night
I'm finally called on to give
the few crumpled regulars
a rousing rendition of
I Did It Their Way:
a little something
to forget me by.

This Small Obituary

They've yet to offer me
a visiting professorship at Oxford or Yale.
And still no sign of the Nobel Prize.
I'll be almost famous in a small town sort of way.
Your next-door neighbour will vaguely remember me,
when some hypocrite writes this small obituary:
"He had a real knack for last lines,
but fell in love with his own invective;
became such an expert at cutting throats,
that, in the end, he slit his own."

TWO

Ponders End

St. Petersburg Scenes

August. The small white cat
in the Winter Palace courtyard
is grabbing all the summer she can get;
as a woman takes time out
from her big loud ice-cream to tell
what looks like her husband
that the Smolny Institute is a place
where someone did something once,
but now it's a girls school. Later,

an old man plays chess against himself
at a bus-stop on Nevsky Prospect;
as the guide book reliably informs us
that above the hotel opposite
sits a plaque: *Leningrad, City of Heroes*
but all we can see
is a Coca Cola sign. And

on the other bank of the Neva,
as the day whitens, a man, whose
role in his own Bolshevik fairytale
has long since earned him a place
on the FBI's least wanted, waits
at the window of Lenin's study
for the disposable camera's
immortalising click; fumbles
in his pockets like a best man
who's mislaid that speech, and gazes
meaningfully into the past.

Kronstadt, Winter Song

The Gulf of Finland hammers
    the fortress walls,
until its voice is silenced too
    under the plain slab
of an Arctic tomb; and ghost insurgents
    wander the white,
chasing remembered sparks
    of Aurora.

My Militant Tendency

It's nineteen eighty two and I know everything.
Hippies are people who always end up asking
Charles Manson to sing them another song.
I'd rather be off putting some fascist through
a glass door arseways, but being fifteen,
have to mow the lawn first. Last year,

Liverpool meant football; now
it's the Petrograd of the British Revolution.
Instead of masturbation, I find socialism.
While others dream of businessmen bleeding
in basements; I promise to abolish double-chemistry class
the minute I become Commissar. In all of this
there is usually a leather jacket involved. I tell

cousin Walter and his lovely new wife, Elizabeth,
to put their aspirations in their underpants
and smoke them; watch

my dad's life become a play:
Sit Down In Anger.

To Curran's Hotel, Eyre Square, Galway

'Electrical, Engineering and Plumbing Trade Union
branch meetings moved to Tonery's Bar, 98 Bohermore'
   —notice pinned to door 3-7-02

Religiously each week,
the endless Coke and *Polo* mints
of impending world revolution. At fifteen,
homework knocked aside by your

insurrectionary video-nights: *Reds,*
October: Ten Days That Shook The World.
He who had the youth apparently having
the future. While on the wall

—Connaught Champions, 1974—
some ancient darts team all saying:
cheese. Guest-speakers eclipsed
by the mouth at the back

with 'something to add.' All this
sent south, as demolition men make of you
a collapse of dust and rotten timber.

And it's like watching the opposition's
last moth-eaten follower being
finally taken out and shot.

Littlehampton

Like falling down several flights of stairs now
to a world gone as the Brixton riots
or "Maggie! Maggie! Maggie! Out! Out! Out!"
Our answers easy and fast as fish 'n chips twice
at the end of the night. Unanimity, as ever,
on the mathematical impossibility of you
                        twenty years on
giving the lawn
its requisite short-back-and-sides,
the gardens of Littlehampton all
standing to attention by the rich
green Lord Tennyson sea.

The Man in The Horsham Computer Room

The day on the verge of its first *Kit Kat*,
when Sanity texts you to say
the grumpy old jumper you've become; and how
being forced to listen to your one man
protest against unfairness in general since
shortly before the big bang
has left her with nowhere to go
but away. By lunchtime

she's ancient history;
as you wax nostalgic on a haircut
that never was.
By close of business you've abandoned
your safety first mineral water
forever; given your worldly goods
to the undeserving; and changed your name
to Dionysus Jones III...

Years later, you return
from your charmed life
as a madman shouting in a toilet
to this movie in which everyone gets laid
but you. And the room's loud with advice
about evening classes in botany
or Bavarian clog-dancing, and how
to make the most of your new job
strangling wild hogs with your bare hands;
when all you want to do is talk
about what it is, in that bit of blue sky,
you remember.

Leaving The World

You left the world to its ordinary onions
    and take-out teas to stay
indoors forever crowning yourself
    Emperor at Notre Dame. Ecstasies of imagined hands
giving you around-the-clock applause for weeks
    in a room pink with pornography and slowly
filling up with smoke. Coming around always
    to the absence of caffeine. The man in the mirror
looking like someone with a hot date
    with the state pathologist: that jaw
you could open a tin of beans with, that hair
    like something nasty from the bottom of the canal.
Your tan leather jacket in the end just vanishing
    through the automatic doors
of an average Saturday.

Ponders End

The night the cat cut her wrists
and the cauliflower cheese you'd been flirting with
since 1979 caught the last bus
to Ponders End, you knew it was time
to get the underpants on, the bicycle moving

and leave your impossible room
and weekly allowance
from the Department of Public Happiness
to themselves; to finally take your secret theory
that a rising boat lifts all skirts

into the Shanghai traffic with the shocked mouth
of a man who expects to be quietly
strangled by evil pragmatists
in broad daylight.

Death of a Revolutionary: Ted Grant (1913-2006)

The last time I saw you
I was twenty five. You were the old coat
at the edge of the demo, saying 'No!';
your plastic bag
still packed with propaganda,
but the world going the other way.

Now, your legendary tea mug
finally stands at ease.
The morning papers come,
but you do not open them.
About the bombs now
demolishing Baalbek and Tyre,
you have nothing to say.

The past is a Northern seaside town in winter;
the cheap hotel, the abandoned pier.
You on a platform jabbing the air,
haranguing the boy I was: "Comrades,
we live in a period of sharp
turns and sudden changes."
My every thought, part
of your master-plan.

The future is the match between Switzerland
and the Ukraine, which rattles
away on a distant TV.
I sit by the water
in this town of Sunday painters.
I do not say, as you did:
"We have kept the faith."

Conversation with a Former Self

Not for you New York or Paris,
a career, perhaps, depicting fashionable
women in their boudoirs. Instead
the bare chapel of your garage flat;

the sour milk and lavender; watching
the cups crack like marriages. You always
a deserving cause rattling its box. The vast,
unforgiving tundra of your politics

stretching on 'til posterity
has your legacy
                    crumpled in its fist:
the bible-studies righteousness
and way you let the world
mop the floor with your head,

until it was a simple case of go quietly
on that pink ladies mountain bike,
or be taken away in this brown
paper-bag.

Political Oblivion

The fifty votes you got may have been
the political equivalent of a woman whispering:
"Is it in yet?" when it's long since been and gone;
but you still smile like an up-and-coming Congressman
slipping into a closet with the Governor of Ohio's wife.

Dad

On yellow evenings
in a country which no longer exists,
we ignore each other
over deceased cups of coffee.
Until I shatter
the pristine silence:
announce my opposition
to the trickledown theory, or
the concept of right and wrong
as you understand it; or say
all things considered
this would be a good time for
the world to end.

Sometimes you bark back:
that in my world without rules
Ian Brady would probably tour Europe
promoting his autobiography
Everybody Gets What They Deserve:
"The author will be available afterwards
to take children from the audience";
and never mind the big opinions,
with my Leaving Cert the only job
I'm fit for, in a country
which no longer exists, is meeting men
in hotels for small change.

But mostly you abscond to give
some innocent shrub
a skinhead haircut; allow me
to keep contradicting myself
until I find out what it is
I'm trying to say.

Family Dispute

Like a Galway team from the Seventies
who, on the last Sunday of September,
were most of the way there,
but blew our promised half-day
in the last fifteen minutes;

at the age of fifty one
and a half, you throw it away
for a hot front seat something
with a neighbour
the old you had nicknamed
Bring Me Your Huddled Asses;

become a bewildered look
in an old white Mercedes. The day
the *FOR SALE* sign goes up on the business
you paint on the side of the building
in angry white letters:
   FAMILY DISPUTE
   KEEP OUT !

After that you cease to exist,
are just a rumour
your enemies sometimes put about;
the sad man in the caravan
who keeps coming back
at me in poems.
My late father.

Memory

Years now since the plaque which read:
"God, in his wisdom, made us a family" leapt
laughing to its kitchen floor death. And yet,
father, here you are: that cusp summer 1974

slipping out the back with a black plastic bag
into a garden thick with thistles and August
to put the kitten we'd cuddled nearly to bits
—whimpering, whimpering—out of its misery.

The History Of Sad

Again listening to you tossing
real people off imaginary tower-blocks;
your tongue's catastrophic slug-in-salt wiggle;
easy to miss what's plain

as a knock on the door in the middle of the day:
you mad to go on carrying crippled dogs
up impossible hills, saddest man
in the history of sad.

Hypothetical Tea

Easy to forget as the waitress wipes
away the curried chips that finally
sent you off down the corridor
in a long tin box, and your voice
is suddenly wind gone out
under a thousand toilet doors;
       the years

we spent trying to invent
a universe where the things you said
made some sort of sense; that being your pal
was pleasurable as nettles
and *Vaseline*, or living
with Liza Minnelli; how in the end
       you were less

a man, than a mildewed suit dreaming always
of being fed to hawks, and that peace,
in practice, meant never meeting you
for that hypothetical tea, now
       that in death

you're not content
to be a small groan from a far room,
but instead insist on being this
orchestra of car-alarms
       at four a.m.

THREE

Firewood

The World Socialist Party
of Honeysuckle Heights

Their weekly meeting is a wide dining table
around which pairs of sandals gather
to have a brittle woman explain how
that sculpture student, who last Wednesday
expressed his anti-imperialism by turning up late
and smelling of fish, is a concrete example
of what Lenin meant when he said
that the tops of the trees move first.
Later, she reassures them, as the crowd thins
that revolution is a great consumer
of human raw material. Until

even the ornaments on the sideboard
begin to make their excuses;
the dusty grandfather clock
waves the comrades goodbye; and she admits
this is no timetable adjustment.
The coming epoch of struggle
has been cancelled. *Thank you.*
And goodnight. Leaving them to pose
for one last photograph. Less the vanguard
of the proletariat, than a dinner party
that kept not happening.

Betrayals

When the bombers refused to turn
into butterflies, and the Workers
went down the road chanting,
"They say fight-back!
We say cut-back!"

she put on her
stop-doing-that-now face
and counterattacked with evening
after evening of pure thoughts
and proper posture; accompanied

her gluten-free muesli
to the veranda and watched the seagulls
flying towards her;
as she took out and weighed
all our betrayals.

Social Realist Poetess Celebrates Birthday

All is well. As the pundits predicted
overnight she turned sixty.
The napkins have reported for duty.
The wine is unremarkable;
but the duck good;
the apple tree by the window
doing exactly what's expected of it,
when her brother-in-law quips:
he thought by now she'd be in Stockholm
turning down the Nobel Prize.

The wine glasses stop moving.
Cousin Basil's bow-tie eyes the exit.
The apple tree doesn't know
where to put its face. The poetess
looks as if she's about to grab
her best tweed hat,
and hurry off to address
a mass-meeting of teamsters,

to reassure the brethren
that she will not rest
until the last postmodernist
has been dispatched
to a bone meal factory
the other side of Mullingar;

and when she's finished
be carried shoulder high
by the horn honking brothers of Local 319
as she leads them in the chant:
"Things as they are! Things as they are!"

The Cause

Diminished now as a seaside town
at the season's close. But still his
pickaxe voice rips the High Street
as it has since he changed his name
to something, which roughly translated
from the old Irish means
'bringer of spasms'.

Each morning he decides
what he's against today,
puts on that screaming red beret
and goes; is years past the point
where the campaigner became
the mad fucker with the sign;

and though there's more truth
in any Andy Williams song
than in what's left of his manifesto;
it's the only break he gets from writing
anonymous threatening letters
to himself, as he nibbles the firelighters
under the rusty ironing-board
he now calls home.

Ending Up

Outside the Burger King on Piccadilly Circus
that's where I met him first, always itching
to quote *Socialism or Catastrophe*
but *Homage to Catalonia* was his favourite book.
In different times he'd have died in Spain.
In the autumn of '88 he married her instead;
ended up on the Essex side of the M25.

In his prime he'd talk all night
—how it would all have been so different—
"if only Rosa Luxembourg took my advice."
I got his dog-eared copy
of *The Ragged Trousered Philanthropists*
the day he went into human resource management;
his *Communist Manifesto* the day he boarded the plane
for a piece of the action on the new Moscow stock exchange.

Their marriage was one of those rare soap operas
which no-one bothers to watch—
the acting wooden, the dialogue nonsensical—
in the end they stayed together;
kept those perfect carpets
out of the divorce courts.
Everything was in order
that Tuesday evening last October.
He took his shoes off, as usual,
at the front door.

Somewhere between the end
of *The Channel Four News*
and the signature tune for *Friends*—
in a matter of seconds—
he went without a struggle;

was dead in the chair
when she got out of the shower;
had one of those English funerals
with no-one at them. A curtain opened
and he was smoke.

Catastrophe comes in many guises
and not always with the strident voice
of a doomed member of the Baader-Meinhoff.
It also arrives, more quietly,
on the Essex side of the M25.

The Great Depression

Since love took its clown questions
and vomit-coloured clothes down
the fire escape that dusk, the woman,
who once put the *quois*
into Je ne sais quois, has gone
from the city of caffeine
and glittering websites
                              to wander late
the boulevards of Stalintown handing
out yellow-pack tuna fish to the poor, her face
like a ruined bank-holiday weekend, her talk
like LSD and downers in a country
where it's always Tuesday.

Original Bohemian Writes To
Ex-Boyfriend About Astronomy

The kitchen's too big and the neighbours are noisier
since the taxi-driver from the Ivory Coast,
I invited back for coffee,
took my Moving Hearts LPs
and vanished into the vast
smoke-free future.

I am a book of complaints
in a town that loves its sushi
and minimalist furniture,
but doesn't do bad news.

This letter is all there is, light
from an extinguished star:
a message reaching you
too late.

Page From The Diary Of An Officially Approved Person

By day, your new blonde hair
and state-sponsored smile are twin planks
in the Government's anti-poverty strategy,
as you put on your enthusiasm and treat
another seminar
to an orgy of flip-charts; then play
Mayors and Ministers off
against each other
over the much anticipated beef stroganoff.
No-one noticing the names being underlined in red
in the twilit Politburo of your mind.

By night, you sit alone in a mansion called *Equality*,
and listen to the moans,
from some far basement, of those
whose nervous hands questioned
this expense account,
that clerk's timely suicide; openly defied
whole conference-loads of otherwise
unanimous applause.

The Candidate

Who, without opening his mouth, tells you
that, for him, it was stay there forever
making up worlds that will never be
in a side-street with nothing to offer
but the monthly *Tea-dance and sing-along
for the over fifty-fives*, or grow up to be
Junior Minister for Counter-Terrorism;

that you can scowl all you want,
his suit will just keep beaming back, now
the miracle of modern dentistry has given the boy
with the shrieking red t-shirt
and mouthful of bombed-out teeth
this ice white New Labour smile;

that as you stand there,
looking suddenly old in the Post Office queue
used, by now, to the idea of not being played
by Jack Nicholson in the film of your life
that'll never be made;

he daydreams he's signing the order
that'll send you away across the courtyard
to have your head shaved
by the Anti-Everything Police.

From Grosvenor Square to Here

Sentences that run on and on,
like a hacking cough. Exclamation
marks which can be seen coming
a mile off, as you load them onto
your machine gun tongue and fire!
You've hawked that suitcase
full of broken old slogans all the way
from Grosvenor Square to here.
Your imagination now a cluttered
basement. By the time you sit down
no-one will be in any doubt,
if rigormortis could talk
this is how it would sound.

Reasons for doing the John Walker Lindh

*"John Walker Lindh, a 20-year-old Californian, was captured while
fighting for the Taliban."* CNN

Because there must be more
to life than basketball;
Habitat for Inhumanity; and
marrying women named Sue
as in *for damages*. Because
your parents increasingly sound
like strange beings from
a far, plastic universe.

Because you'd rather go
where the coffins are leaky
and the summers hot, fight
the bad fight at Mazaar-E-Shariff,
than suffer another Level 5 Christmas
at the *Radisson*, or be remembered
as someone who overcame huge
advantages to achieve
total obscurity.

Firewood

A bone field fifty metres by fifty.
It's problematic to describe this as genocide.
I gather firewood at eight o'clock in the morning.
My son clings to my dress. Men in uniforms
with military insignia stop their car
and throw him into a fire. Then five of them
one after the other. I am paralysed.
It's problematic to describe this as genocide.
The solution is not military intervention. We demand
the US keep its hands off Sudan.
Children start jumping out windows
when the Janjaweed come into the school.
The police begin firing. Everyone,
mainly babies and the elderly,
falls down. I am standing on bodies.
A military barracks.
No bathroom. People stay still,
suffering their wounds.
People stay still. No bathroom.
A military barracks. I am standing on bodies,
fall down. Mainly babies and the elderly.
Everyone. The police begin firing.
When the Janjaweed come into the school,
children start jumping out windows.
The solution not military intervention.
The US keep its hands off Sudan, we demand
It's problematic to describe this as genocide.
I am paralysed. One after the other,
five of them. They stop their car
and throw him into a fire. Men
in uniforms with military insignia.
My son clings to my dress.
At eight o'clock in the morning I gather firewood.
It's problematic to describe this as genocide.
A bone field fifty metres by fifty.

* The non-italicised lines are quotations from eye-witness accounts from Darfur

The Annual Air Show Protest

U.S. Air Force Thunderbirds are God
taking pneumatic drills to the sky.
The cat covers his ears and retires
to the back of the wardrobe.
Elsewhere, a demo gives old friends
somewhere to put their anger.
The man, who every chance he gets
ticks you off for bearing false witness
against East Germany, hands out red balloons.
His moustache stops to congratulate itself.
His heartbeat hammers: Long Live Stalin!
Long Live Stalin! A guy with purple hair
offers Food Not Bombs to an elderly
white woman with dreadlocks.

You uproot weeds, tell yourself
if their dream republic got born,
the cat wouldn't be crouching
in the dark, but cold between slices
of questionable brown bread
—all you'd have to eat—know
you're more likely to go
into the night on a unicycle
screaming: Free Paris Hilton!
Free Paris Hilton! than accept
another red balloon from them.

FOUR

A New City

A New City

To think of you, exiled there
among the three-bar-fires
and broken toilet seats of Bohemia;
not as we who imagined we'd finally

sent you to Alcatraz all had it:
spiders and mice riddling
your beard as, night after night,
you clawed the door; but

on a long-suffering cushion
your imagination hammering somehow
from old news and orange peel,
two decade's rubble and scrap,
brick by brick: a new city.

Summer Interlude

And then from nowhere
a morning long and mellow
as a white cat stretched across a hot window;
birdsong ringing out across suburbia,
like bells celebrating a famous victory.
Nothing for the already shortening days
but to put them aside,
and just listen to the symphony:
for not quite fifteen minutes
life seeming set to stay
suspended forever
there in high July.

Shannon Airport, October 21st, 2002

Now beginning our descent
trading "all we have is hundred dollar bills"
for a definite dose of the nasal drip.
But remember
      on Central Park the trees
like sprinkled broccoli, the evening
traffic a spangled centipede
down the Avenue of the Americas:
that City of hot dogs and glittering geometry.
      Fuel enough
to carry us through afternoons bitter
as black tea and one cream-cracker each,
nights severe as a nun's whisper
in a small boy's ear.

Living Proof

for Susan

The poet, who this time twenty years ago was busy
failing English in the Leaving Cert, waits
at the end of an aisle for the woman,
who by dinner time will be his
new American wife; remembers
on this best June day, the night
he boarded the bus at the end of a previous life,
where he was just a throwaway remark
in a kebab shop on West Green Road; living proof
that if you keep not trying eventually
it won't happen. This best June day.
The sun extravagant, the music starting to play ...

She Considers His Proposal

Yes is a place where it's okay
that his parties are always bring your own
      toilet-brush affairs; that on
bank holiday Mondays he talks
      to her through the bathroom door
about the phone bill; that loyalty might mean
      being dragged before a tribunal
to answer questions about a scam
      perpetuated by him. That his wallet
is crammed with membership-cards
      of clubs that threw him out.

That her shoes have been stolen
      by rodents. Yes is a place
it's okay that he must tell her once more
      how when he was small,
his mother would sometimes soak
      the whole family in *Dettol*.
That he never overcame his fear
      of cottage cheese.

That when things go wrong he turns to her
      and says: "just because I'm kicking
imaginary people in the testicles
      doesn't mean we can't hold hands."
That each morning he tells her:
      "If you were just a pair of eyebrows,
I'd still be here looking at you."
      Yes is a place it's okay.

Warming Your Hands

As outside the hailstones come
and the wind goes on and on
like an old man at a bus–stop, you think
about going to work. Until

just one glimpse of her
further and better particulars
persuades you instead
to spend the afternoon

warming your hands
on the three-bar
fire of her arse.

The Cat's Point of View: A Prose Poem

for Karma

It's hardly surprising she hates having her temperature taken.
I mean, how would you like it, if some people you'd never seen
before in your life suddenly stuck a huge glass tube up your
backside for no apparent reason? The last time that happened
to me I found it very disturbing indeed. *And the bastards
never even came up with the money.* I chased them for weeks,
but it was a complete waste of time.

Absence

When you go, I'm a boy
lost in enormous shorts;
the news remains untranslated:
Chinese Muslims and lesbian bishops.

Breakfast is a bowl
of socialist sounding lies;
my old pal, Truth, welcome
as a hot coffee
in the balls.

Each morning I write offering
Osama Bin Laden a pact
(but he keeps not answering my letters)
then browse my favourite website:
Cats that look like Hitler.

When you go
childhood is a field full of hay
that was never that golden.

The story so far amounts
to a short history of
hardly anything

when you go.

Too Close To Call: Results Party, 2004

The early promise of an evening hot
with dancing and lesbianism gives way
to us remaining few chewing the lino
as the loud open fire goes quiet,
and the last plate of hot dogs sits
       apocalyptically
on our electoral map of America.

Until all the networks agree
the latest from Ohio seems to indicate
the President's face has stopped twitching.
And somewhere in darkest Wyoming
Dick Cheney sits down to a celebratory breakfast
of lambs' testicles and *Aspirin*; while here the sun
arrives white and useless at the window
on this day of so much Champagne still pink
and unopened in the fridge.

Extra

No part of anyone's plan. One
dark afternoon God doodled
on His copybook and
nine months later
he was born. Forty
years on and still the blank
page of his face
with, at its centre, a tiny
little question-mark; the mouth
he keeps moving to hide
the nothing going on in his head
apart from one embarrassing silence
after another. The one who turns up
as an extra at the edge
of every couple's arguments,
with nothing to do but hold
the stopped wristwatch of his life,
as he smiles, like a bald man whose shiny
new hair just arrived in the post,
and mutters to himself: who needs love
when you've got
the musty cheese sandwich that lives
in the dark away of your raincoat?

Wholesale Clearance: Everything Must Go

Into the carpeted conference room we go
to listen to a bloke, whose rhetoric
is Del Boy meets Billy Graham, tell us
to lay down our wallets and walk,
"Ladies and gentlemen", not towards
The Lord Jesus, but this set
of twenty pots and pans; this pair
of high powered binoculars, he says
will be *the business* on
that topless beach next July;
this electric toothbrush,
reserve price: € 3.99… Until the guy

who bought the binoculars
shouts to let us know:
the traffic backed up along
the interstate highway of his Aorta
has stopped moving; the motorists
have abandoned their SUVs, and gone
bargainless and roaring
in all directions. We crowd

to glimpse his surprise
as he lets go
of what probably began
in the back of an old Ford Anglia
circa 1962; learn later
he spent his life
in pest control.

Where Christmas Went

Though you hate to use the word useless;
the year Dad got a coffin for Christmas
—three decades after he gave up work
to do a PhD in whiskey—
all that changed was the national debt
decreased slightly and
the Chancellor of the Exchequer revised
his forecast for growth
upwards. Even now,

despite the roast quail, the apple brandy,
you move among the crowd in the Café Nero
with the face of a man who would sell out
but can't find a buyer. And Christmas
doesn't mean Him, but what a boy
named a dog he found sniffing
the back streets of Hackney.

Where it went,
        you still follow.

Keyser Soze Does Not Frighten Me

When your mother walks
in on us with her fallen arches,
her irritable bowel and pernicious anaemia,
her tales of endless samples taken in endless jars;
and is no sooner in the door than there
she sits with the medical dictionary,
moving her fingers lovingly across its pages:
Colostomy, Phallectomy, Bubonic Plague,
I sometimes think: while they're not looking
I should make a run for it, could be
at the airport before anyone missed me;
would manage somehow, try my hand at anything,
perhaps drive a taxi in Islamabad,
herd goats in Mongolia, be last heard of
running rackets in Atlantic City,
before vanishing off the face of the earth;
because Keyser Soze does not frighten me,
but I'm scared to death of her.

A Previous Engagement

At seven a.m. what sounds
like him upstairs being loudly
eaten by angry greyhounds, as morning crashes
through the curtains like a man
who'd be happy to beat your head in
with a metal pipe, no questions asked. You

with the hairdo commonly known
as government spending-cut, and small voice
of someone, who expects his testicles
to drop off (plop, plop, goodnight) any moment now.
The tower-block muttering
into its daily gruel. And the girl

you'd seemed destined to sweep down the aisle
to a life of shouting and insomnia, next door
tearing the wallpaper, as you go anywhere
                                        to sit
with your no tier wedding cake and head
full of the previous week; alone again
in the red room of you.

Infatuation

Was long ago swallowed
by those satanic herds that seethed back and forth
across the malicious scowl of a winter sea.

I'm frozen to the bone,
how I need a warm coat.

And I trekked far away under an empty sky
which, starless and moonless,
had nothing much to say for itself,
except the endless rattle
of a wretched wind.

I'm frozen to the bone,
how I need a warm coat.

These eyes see it all in black and white,
they're blind to the brilliance
which colours the measureless.

These shoulders struggle
under tyrannical weights,
as I grind through the streets
to find my escape.

I'm frozen to the bone,
how I need a warm coat.

Word From The Other Country

Where you've gone
      the air may be a Mardi Gras
of insects and pollen,
      but where I live
it's winter. World without ice cream,
      Amen.
I make do with soda bread,
      and spend long evenings
googling you. Most days,
      I know
it was nothing personal:
      I was the hobby
you took up to pass
      the worst years
of the recession. And when
      the sky comes down
I still rush out to take
      your favourite T-shirt
in out of the rain.

FIVE

Last Testament

A New Calendar

The Sunday papers and then
the packed lunch, the polished shoes
work hanging over everything, like a news
report naming a hundred and twenty different types
of tumour, tempered only by bright
intervals in the south and west.

Even your dreams, less the usual array
of dazzling blondes wandering through,
like lush metaphors for something else,
than an inexorable walk down by the hospital
past telephones ringing in empty houses.
And waking now

to an alarm angry as a black-backed jackal.
You there, with your grim cheese slices,
your tar-like tea, not liking the look,
smell, texture or sound of anything; as outside
a new calendar's first Monday comes,
like a dentist's drill, screaming to a start.

Careful Driver

He's the husband who promised the earth
but ended up giving her
a bad week in Bognor Regis.
And rather than go

where breakfast's sometimes
what remains of the sandwich
you took to bed last night, the only light a candle
made of earwax donated
by your last flat-mate but one; or perhaps

become the guy
in the yellow jumpsuit and pale blue shoes,
who always ends the night screaming
about the Confederate flag the Lady Mayoress
keeps in her attic; he lives out

the rest of his death in this wastepaper basket.
The first man in history killed
by too much careful driving.

The Doctor's Waiting Room

Outside, a train somewhere hammering its tracks,
as he looks back
on your Mickey Mouse socks
and list of men who left in the rain
without flushing the toilet;
sees himself across a room
full of cheap polyester suits.
That small conformist waiting to be born.
And after the honeymoon

one day waking up
in a country ruled by you.
Your road-rage face,
strategic tears and apologies always,
like artificial Los Angeles snow.
Him late, breathless and red faced as ever.
You taking the world warmly by the throat.
All the way

to a day such as this
—the buses coming and going,
the post unopened on the mat—
and him left remembering them well
by that waiting room wall: all the Au Pairs
and neighbours' wives
he might've absconded with
but didn't; as he waits

for the man to say
more this time than a simple: "take two
three times daily" or "apply
the ointment to the infected area
and rub in gently."

Your Ideal Friday Night

I hear what you say;
but as once again you sit
with your backside buried
in that chair there, your face
like months and months of pent up rain
all falling on the same day;
can you blame me for thinking,
that deep down you'd probably prefer
another evening in with the local rag:
*"Man Who Once Crossed Littlehampton High Street
Did Absolutely Nothing Yesterday"*:
to a hundred hot nights with Samantha Mumba;
that your ideal Friday night is watching
the mildew advance across an old coat,
as you wait for your bones
to go finally cold?

Woman On The Verge Of Sending Husband Quietly To Hell

Your hospital face as we say goodbye
to the last of August and sandcastles. You now
a rumbling stomach with a silly haircut,
waiting for something to come
out of thin, inspirational air. Tomorrow,
        I'll leave you
to drink cups of cold tea through a straw
on your premium quality wooden toilet seat, and pen
your autobiographical masterpiece:
Tribute To A Nonentity. But tonight,
        Hell's still empty
except for a nightwatchman, waiting.

The Boy

Who in the crystal ball saw
cheering crowds in the Stadium of Light,
a life spent diving between
various women's electric thighs, now
settling his *Best Buttocks, 1975* across
an executive chair's second-hand leather,
like some pipe-smoking, pot-bellied,
small-time God. On the verge just then
of an important thought,

but no. That *Brillo* pad beard,
that joke-shop nose signalling
his unsung glamour's
sad supplanting. Tonight for sure
the impossibility of sleep, and then
in dreams to wander the bombed out palace
of his old ambitions. The clean steel

and rusty thumb-tacks
of all those different accents nailing
the blame, as his ripening
haemorrhoids once more
take off on a bicycle
made for none.

Shapeless Days Shuffling

Constant as stopped clocks or money
under the mattress. Your weak tea,
discoloured secrets and voice like snow through
a sulk black afternoon. The shapeless days shuffling
your serviceable drawers once more down the hallway,
like a minor character in one of Jane Austen's
lesser known novels. Until with its high pitched laugh
the universe signals not last minute Valentines
in big red envelopes—some cut-price Napoleon
in the end maybe taking you to the gates of Moscow—
but coming cobweb hair and rumours of cat food:
the slow multiplication of all your small disappointments
into the bound volumes of broken promises
opening nightly now across the mahogany.

Portrait of the Boss Shaking
Hands with Himself

So busy shaking hands with yourself
you miss in children's laughter
the universe warning you; never get it
when sidekicks leave post-its saying:
"Gone to live in North Korea",
or suggest your strategy

for the next shareholders' meeting should be
to do a little interpretive dance
to *"Fanny (Be Tender With My Love)"*
by the Bee Gees; nor spot
all around you briefcases fondly

remembering poverty—Spanish whiskey
on collapsing afternoons—and dreaming,
as once more they wave you off on holiday,
of a white mini-bus going off the motorway,
an Hawaiian shirt finally quiet.

December

Something ending.
And not, as expected, with a string quartet,
but a ceremony desperate
as a *Spam* sandwich trapped
in an old man's mouth.

Tomorrow no longer
when you maybe get to play Carnegie Hall,
but a number Six bus taking you back
to the wood panelling's slow collapse:
the ghost of mildew yet to come.

By day shuffling sideways at breakneck speed.
By night bronchitis and a small TV offering
all the wagging well kept beards
and fitness equipment you
could possibly want.

Retirement

The word you thought meant: time to tend the tulips
and perhaps, like your father, in later life develop
a big Dublin accent and definite knack of telling it
like it isn't; or summering by the seaside

where you'd employee as a manservant
a chimpanzee called Harold, and sometimes
leave your false teeth in the taxi after a weekend
corrupting young people in late night places

turns out to mean: sitting here (your eyes gone out
like candles) as the whiskey-voiced nurse reads aloud
from *The Daily Mirror*, and you remember

when life was something dreamt up at a bus-stop
on the outskirts of Athlone by a young fool
who thought the rain would stop soon.

Last Testament

Whether I leave this world peacefully,
surrounded by respectable nephews
and voluptuous nieces, or go roaring
at four in the morning in the Prison Hospital,
come what may, let no black crow
sit squawking by my bed,
but pin this sign above my head:
"This fucker here does not repent,
would do the same again and worse."
Yes, when I have gasped my final gasp,
let Satan clap his hands and cry: "At last!"
May I be down below, having
dinner with Tricky Dicky, sharing
dirty jokes with old Al Haig;
before "nice Father What's-
His-Name" realises I'm gone.

Hospital

In the back gate and past
the giant red brick chimney;
through whispering doors to where
a woman with a skilled smile takes
your details at a desk and sends you
—a small boy again—into that world
of thin men in dressing gowns. A corridor
you go down for blood or cancer;
a toilet, where from the ceiling hangs
a chord you pull to tell them it's time
you were driven away from here by a blank man
in a hearse with no licence plates.